BR Colour Album

L.A. NIXON

First published in the United Kingdom in 1983 by
Jane's Publishing Company Limited
238 City Road, London EC1V 2PU

ISBN 0 7106 0287 1

Printed by Toppan Printing Co (S) Pte Ltd
38 Liu Fang Road, Jurong, Singapore 2262

JANE'S

Cover illustrations

Front: class 37 No 37112, one of Eastfield's allocation in 1982 to receive the short lived experimental livery of wrap-around yellow noses, makes light work of the four-coach 1254 Glasgow Queen Street–Oban as it heads up Strath Fillan against the majestic backdrop of Ben More on 13 April 1982. (*David Nixon*)
Pentax 6 × 7   200 mm Takumar   Ektachrome 200 1/500, f5.6

Rear: class 86/2 No 86256 *Pebble Mill* runs across the viaduct into Stockport on 25 March 1983 with the 1613 Manchester Piccadilly–Euston.
Pentax 6 × 7   200 mm Takumar   Ektachrome 200 1/250, f6.3

Right: a contrasting selection of motive power seen through the breakdown crane at Crewe South depot on 18 July 1982 includes class 33 No 33033, class 81 25 kV electric No 81014 and class 474 No 47447.
Leica M3   50 mm Summilux   Kodachrome 25   1/60, f6.3

Introduction

The first Jane's album of colour photographs *British Rail in Colour* was enthusiastically received, but it was acknowledged that in a collection of 100 pictures it could be nothing more than a dip into the vast pool of available material. The task of selecting the photographs for this second album has been particularly pleasant, not least because of the wealth of material which has been made available to me. Indeed I would like to take this opportunity to thank all those who have been kind enough to loan me often invaluable pictures from their collections.

Inevitably I have had to exclude many even though they were of exceptional technical and pictorial merit but my aim has been to present a national survey of the modern BR scene which complements the earlier volume.

Once again I have selected a number of views of the early days of BR non-steam traction to provide in many cases a striking contrast with today's still fascinating and varied motive power scene.

Some may be disappointed by the absence of a favourite operation, locomotive or location but I trust all readers will find something of interest in the following pages.

In response to many requests, photographic technical details, where known, are presented as footnotes to captions.

As before, photographs not credited are the work of the compiler.

In conclusion I would like to thank Ken Harris at Jane's for allowing me complete freedom of choice of material and of layout, and to my wife Carol who, once again, has provided an efficient typing service and tolerated my many hours by the lineside.

L. A. NIXON
Hathersage
June 1983

Opposite. 'Western' diesel-hydraulic No D1015 *Western Champion*, wearing the rather attractive but short-lived golden ochre livery, charges Hatton Bank with a Paddington–Birmingham (Snow Hill) and Wolverhampton (Low Level) express in May 1963. (*Peter Hughes*)
Leica M3   50 mm Summilux   Kodachrome II

Above. Crompton class 33s Nos 33032 and 33042 pool their efforts as they head up the delightful Wylye Valley near Great Wishford with an empty Amey Roadstone train on 15 April 1983. This pleasant cross-country line, linking Salisbury and Westbury, is intensively used, with the hourly Portsmouth–Bristol ser-vices punctuated by frequent mineral trains to and from Merehead and Whatley quarries.
Pentax 6 × 7   200 mm Takumar
Ektachrome 200   1/500, f5.6

Above. The coal reserves of many of the collieries in South Yorkshire are now almost exhausted and scenes such as this, where pithead winding gear stand as silent testimony to industrial dereliction, are commonplace. Class 56 No. 56102 eases its train of empty HAA merry-go-round hoppers past the remains of Denaby Colliery, Conisborough on 9 March 1983.
Pentax 6 × 7   150 mm Takumar
Ektachrome 200   1/250, f6.3

Opposite. The class 56s have been associated with the merry-go-round coal traffic of South Yorkshire and the East Midlands since their introduction in 1976. In April 1983 no fewer than 44 were allocated to Tinsley TMD with another 27 based at Toton. The decision to adopt the new style livery for the class has certainly enlivened a somewhat drab scene – much to the delight of railway photographers. Visits to washing plants are few and far between, however, and it is rare to see them in pristine condition. Here No 56095, one of the later batch built at Doncaster, heads past Welbeck Colliery Junction towards Clipstone with a train of empties on 14 May 1982.
Pentax 6 × 7   150 mm Takumar
Ektachrome 200   1/500, f5.6

56 095

Opposite. The line between Starcross and Teignmouth in Devon is one of the more popular haunts of railway photographers. The locations may be familiar but to while away the hours by the sea is a particularly pleasant adjunct to photography. The views from Langstone Rock near Dawlish Warren are quite spectacular, as can be seen in this picture of class 47/4 No 47476 heading an up express on 24 August 1982. (David Nixon)

Pentax 6 × 7   150 mm Takumar
Ektachrome 200   1/500, f6.3

Above. The Crompton class 33s now monopolise the cross country Portsmouth (Harbour)–Bristol/Cardiff services. The route through Southampton, Salisbury, Westbury, Bath and the Severn Tunnel is one of the more interesting rail journeys in Southern England, the industry of South Wales contrasting with the Georgian terraces of Bath and the wide expanses of Salisbury Plain. Here passengers for Portsmouth enjoy a brief glimpse of the bustling marina at Burseldon on the Hamble on 13 April 1983.

Pentax 6 × 7   105 mm Takumar
Ektachrome 200   1/500, f5.6

Left. In recent years one of the more interesting summer Saturdays only trains to South of England seaside resorts is the 0710 Bradford (Exchange)–Weymouth. After departure from the Yorkshire terminus the train is diagrammed to take the former Lancashire and Yorkshire Railway route through Halifax and on to the Calder Valley main line to Bradley Wood Junction. After reversal at Huddersfield the route taken is via Healey Mills, Barnsley, Wincobank Junction and Sheffield. On 14 August 1982 the only named class 46 Peak, No 46026 *Leicestershire and Derbyshire Yeomanry*, made a rare appearance on the return working and the train is seen here nearing journey's end as it emerges from Bowling tunnel, Bradford.
Pentax 6 × 7
150 mm Takumar
Agfa R100S   *1/250, f5.6*

Opposite. With the virtual displacement in 1982 and 1983 of eth class 45 Peaks from their traditional duties on the Midland main line these venerable locomotives are finding a new lease of life on trans-Pennine expresses. Here No 45144 *Royal Signals* starts the long climb from Stalybridge to the summit at Standedge with the 0905 Liverpool Lime Street–Scarborough on 25 September 1982.
Pentax 6 × 7
105 mm Takumar
Agfa R100S   *1/250, f5.6*

Right. If the excellence of a railway is judged by the number of express trains it carries, then the former LNW Euston–Crewe line must be near, if not at, the top of the BR league. Electrification at 25 kV in the 1960s brought with it efficiency and apparently effortless almost silent motive power but, the luckless APT apart, these services are rarely in the headlines. On a windy Sunday afternoon an unidentified class 81 'sparkler' sweeps almost unnoticed through Leighton Buzzard with a down express on 10 April 1983.
Pentax 6 × 7
150 mm Takumar
Ektachrome 200
1/250, f4.5

Opposite. Class 86 No 86235 *Novelty* speeds round the curves in the upper Clyde Valley near Crawford with the combined 1025 Edinburgh and 1045 Glasgow Central–Manchester Victoria express on 16 April 1982. (*David Nixon*)
Pentax 6 × 7
200 mm Takumar
Ektachrome 200
1/500, f5.6

Opposite. Class 40 No 40165 poses for the camera at Aberdeen Ferryhill on 3 September 1976.
Nikon F   85 mm Nikkor
Kodachrome II   1/125, f4.5

Below. Anglo-Scottish Freightliner traffic is undoubtedly a financial success story. Even in the present recession loading statistics are excellent if not quite up to the standards of 1976, the date of this ECML scene. On a beautiful afternoon in early June class 40 No 40157 skirts the North Sea at Lamberton with an up service.
Nikon F   85 mm Nikkor
Kodachrome 25   1/250, f4

The characteristic drone of the Napier 'Deltic' two stroke engines, which for so many years pleasantly disturbed the tranquility of Alnmouth in Northumberland, is no more. In the closing months of its BR service No 55022 *Royal Scots Grey* skirts the sea on the approach to the station with the 0736 Plymouth–Edinburgh. *(David Nixon)*

Pentax 6 × 7   150 mm Takumar
Ektachrome 200   1/500, f5.6

GARVE

For many years class 31s have been the mainstay motive power of summer Saturdays only holiday trains to East Anglian resorts. Disc-fitted No 31102 leads sister locomotive No 31245 with the 1444 Yarmouth–Derby as they accelerate away from Trowse Lower Junction on the cross-country route to Thetford and Ely on 31 July 1982. The viaduct, quite impressive for an East Anglian location, carries the main line to Liverpool Street. (*David Nixon*)
Pentax 6 × 7   150 mm Takumar
Ektachrome 200   1/500, f5.6

A busy Saturday afternoon scene at Norwich Thorpe on 31 July 1982. Class 37 No 37053 leaves with an up parcels train while No 47579 awaits departure with the 1631 to Liverpool Street. It is interesting to reflect that the corresponding picture of July 1992 may well feature 25 kV electric locomotives!

Pentax 6 × 7   200 mm Takumar
Ektachrome 200   1/250, f8

Opposite. Now that passenger trains have totally disappeared from the Dinting–Sheffield section of the Woodhead trans-Pennine line it is interesting to recall that only 13 years ago class 76 1500 volt dc locomotives were the motive power for an hourly inter-city service linking Manchester with Sheffield. Here green-liveried No 76055, formerly *Prometheus*, rolls its 5-coach train over the Wicker bridge and into Sheffield Victoria on a sunny 29 October 1969.
Leica M3   50 mm Summilux
Kodachrome II   1/250, f3.5

Above. In the heart of the Midlands class 85 No 85008 approaches Smethwick with the 0750 Swansea–Manchester on 30 December 1982. The high rise buildings of Birmingham overlook the scene while prominent in the middle distance are the bridge abutments which once carried the branch to Harborne over the Birmingham canal.
Nikon F   85 mm Nikkor
Kodachrome 64   1/250, f4.5

Opposite. 'Hoover' No 50009 *Conqueror* finds itself relegated to mundane ballast train duties on 25 August 1982. The magnificent GWR semaphore signal gantry unmistakably identifies the location as Exeter St Davids but it will soon be no more; the construction of a new power signal box at the south end of the station is already at an advanced stage.
Pentax 6 × 7   150 mm Takumar
Ektachrome 200   1/500, f5.6

Above. Firmly in home territory between St Austell and Par, English Electric class 50s Nos 50004 *St Vincent* and 50028 *Tiger* provide super-power for the 1210 Penzance–Glasgow parcels on 18 January 1983. (*Hugh Ballantyne*)
Leica M4-2   50 mm Summicron
Kodachrome 64   1/500, f2.8

Readers who have access to a copy of our earlier publication *British Rail in Colour* will find it of interest to compare this picture with that featured on page 87. Both photographs were taken from about the same location near Westbourne Park but they are separated by a time interval of 20 years.

In this scene the M40 motorway has yet to appear and maroon 'Westerns' reigned supreme on West of England expresses. No D1049 *Western Monarch* heads a down express comprising chocolate and cream, maroon, and blood and custard stock on 19 October 1963. The block of high rise flats visible above the fourth coach enjoyed a very short life; shortly after construction it was demolished to make way for the motorway. (*R C Riley*)
Agfa Silette   50 mm Solagon
Kodachrome II   1/500, f2

It is now a quarter of a century since the 'Warship' diesel-hydraulics first made their impact on Western Region express passenger services. In this rare photograph No D800 *Sir Brian Robert-son* heads a rake of blood and custard stock, forming the 1320 Penzance–Paddington, at Cowley Bridge Junction, Exeter, on 16 July 1958 during a return demonstration run from London. The headboard reads 'The First 2,000 hp Diesel-Hydraulic Locomotive'. (*R C Riley*)
Agfa Silette   50 mm Solagon
Kodachrome I   1/250, f2.5

NATIONAL CARRIERS
NATIONAL CARRIERS
NATIONAL DISTRIBUTION SERVICE
03086

Opposite. Class 03 No 03086
earns her keep as
she manoeuvres a lengthy
Freightliner at Ipswich on
3 August 1982. The lower
yard at Ipswich was pressed
into use to service extra
Freightliner traffic following
the protracted ASLEF strike
which formally ended on 18
July. Note the match wagon
permanently coupled to the
shunter for track circuiting
purposes.
Nikon F   85 mm Nikkor
Kodachrome 25
1/250, f3.8

Left. Coal trains on the
former Burry Port and
Gwendreath Valley railway
in South Wales for some time
have been handled by a most
unusual combination of
motive power – a trio of class
03 shunters. Because of
loading gauge restrictions
these are the only BR
locomotives allowed on the
branch and even these have
modified cut down cabs. In
this scene, photographed on
19 August 1982, Nos 03151
and 03152, working in
multiple, lead sister
locomotive 03120 on the last
stage of the run into Burry
Port. The reign of the 03s
was however in 1983
drawing to a close; the
completion of a new rail link
from Coedbach washery to
the main line at Kidwelly
was soon to allow the use of
more conventional power.
Pentax 6 × 7
105 mm Takumar
Ektachrome 200
1/250, f6.3

Left. In recent years the sphere of regular activity of the Crompton class 33s has extended well beyond their earlier confines of Southern England, although they continue to be allocated to the traction maintenance depots at Hither Green and Eastleigh. In 1982 they were regular performers through South Wales to Pembrokeshire, north to Hereford and Crewe and they even enjoyed a weekly duty (the FO 1246 Portsmouth–Leeds) as far as Birmingham. An immaculate No 33012 heads the 1715 Swansea–Milford Haven near Kidwelly on 18 August 1982. Note the TPO vans in the train consist. (*David Nixon*)
Pentax 6 × 7
150 mm Takumar
Ektachrome 200
1/500, f5.6

Opposite. The unique character of the Southern Region is very evident in this morning scene at Eastleigh on 13 April 1983. Crompton class 33 No 33062 speeds through with a down empty stock working, while 47361 eases an oil train off the up main line. On the right distinctive English Electric-powered class 205 'Hampshire' diesel-electric multiple unit No 1133 waits for access to the station to form the 1203 to Portsmouth Harbour.
Pentax 6 × 7
150 mm Takumar
Ektachrome 200
1/500, f5.6

DORMAN
LONG

Left. The industrial heartland of Tees-side at South Bank near Grangetown is the impressive setting in this study of class 31 Nos 31163 and 31219 with an eastbound coal haul on 10 May 1983. Dominating the horizon is the famous transporter bridge at Middlesbrough, while in the foreground the redundant sidings and steel ladles of BSC Cleveland bear silent witness to the economic recession.

Pentax 6 × 7   105 mm Takumar
Ektachrome 200   1/250, f8

In 1961 the Brush prototype diesel-electric No D0280 made its first public appearance, and for a period of nine years saw experimental service on both Eastern and Western Regions. Named *Falcon* after the Brush works at Loughborough, it was transferred to BR capital stock in 1971, becoming class 53 and carrying the number D1200. It then eked out its days on secondary duties in South Wales before final withdrawal from service in October 1975. Here the locomotive, in standard BR blue livery, is seen leaving the Uskmouth branch at Uskmouth Junction, Newport on 6 March 1973. (*Ken Harris*)

Zenith E   135 mm Soligor
High Speed Ektachrome

Opposite. The cavernous train shed at York station frames a class 105 Cravens two-car dmu in November 1975.
Leica M3   50 mm Summulux
Kodachrome II

Above. Freak lighting conditions give a million dollar gold-plated appearance to 'Deltic' No 55022 *Royal Scots Grey* westbound with the 1305 Liverpool–York at Marsden on 4 December 1981. (*Robin Lush*)

Nikon F3   85 mm Nikkor
Kodachrome 25   1/250, f3.5

Right. An HST forming a cross-country South West–North East service glides effortlessly up the 1 in 75 bank towards Ashley Down, Bristol on 22 August 1982. The branch seen diverging to the right of the picture serves Severn Beach. Branch services from Temple Meads are usually in the hands of Pressed Steel class 121 single railcars.
Pentax 6 × 7
150 mm Takumar
Ektachrome 200
1/500, f5.6

Opposite. High Speed Trains are now the cornerstone of BR express passenger operations on the Eastern and Western Regions. There can be little doubt that their speed, efficiency, comfort and reliability has done much to improve the image of BR with the travelling public. The enthusiast may find them monotonous but the recent decision to name selected power cars is a welcome development. A Swansea–Paddington service passes the steelworks at Port Talbot on 21 August 1982.
Pentax 6 × 7
200 mm Takumar
Ektachrome 200
1/500, f5.6

Above. A light sprinkling of snow helps to enliven the drab West Riding scene at Gledholt tunnel as a rather unkept 37141 heads up the bank towards Standedge on 7 January 1982. At this time most parts of the country experienced some of the coldest winter weather ever, with over thirty degrees of frost recorded. Certainly the external cleanliness of freight motive power was the very last concern of BR operating staff. Engines severely damaged by frost and frozen fuel lines were just two of the major problems of the day.
Pentax 6 × 7   150 mm Takumar
Ektachrome 200   1/250, f5.6

Opposite. The minimal accommodation now provided for passengers at unstaffed stations is all too evident in this photograph of Dore. It is hard to believe that this station once boasted no fewer than four waiting rooms and of course during the winter months each would have had a blazing coal fire. Here the temperature is well below freezing as 'Peak' No 45135 hurries through with the 0900 St Pancras–Sheffield on 22 December 1982.
Pentax 6 × 7   200 mm Takumar
Ektachrome 200   1/500, f6.3

Below. In superb ex-works condition class 71 electric locomotive No E5012 is bathed in the afternoon sunshine as it stands in Eastleigh Works yard on 1 September 1962. Note the pantograph used to pick up current during shunting operations in goods yards and sidings not equipped with the third rail system. (*Ken Plant*)
Agfa Super Silette   50 mm   Agfa CT18

Opposite. Twenty-five years ago the dockland cranes of the Pool of London and St Pauls dominated the City skyline in contrast with today's high rise office blocks. In this vintage scene of London Bridge station photographed on 17 June 1959, class 71 electric locomotive No E5003 leaves with the 1244 Ramsgate parcels.

This locomotive had quite a chequered career; it was rebuilt as an electro-diesel in 1968 when it was re-numbered E6107. It later carried the computer based number 74007 and was finally withdrawn from traffic in December 1977. (*R C Riley*)
Agfa Silette   50 mm Solagon
Kodachrome I   1/250, f2.8

Left. Photographed from above the tunnel to the south of Guildford station on 30 October 1982 is class 421/2 electric multiple-unit No 7351. Present day visitors are probably unaware that the extensive car park, partly visible at the extreme left of the picture, was once the site of the roundhouse of Guildford steam shed.
Nikon F 85 mm Nikkor
Kodachrome 25 1/125, f2.2

Opposite. Visitors to the Peak District in November are rarely rewarded by weather conditions such as this but no doubt passengers for Sheffield on this two-car class 114 Derby Heavyweight dmu appreciated their good fortune on 13 November 1976.

The photograph was taken from the lower slopes of Loose Hill in Edale, which affords superb panoramic views of the railway in a Pennine moorland setting.
Leica M3 50 mm Summilux
Kodachrome II 1/125, f4.5

OVERLEAF

Left. The whisky industry, long associated with the Speyside area of north-east Scotland, influenced the development of railways in the area. Today except for the Keith–Aberdeen line little remains of the once extensive Great North of Scotland system and trains serving the whisky distilleries are few and far between. One survivor in 1982 was this train which, on weekday afternoons, left the Chivas distribution terminal at Keith (ironically situated on the site of the old steam shed) for Aberdeen and points south. At today's prices this must be one of the most valuable commodities carried by British Rail. Class 27 No 27109 was photographed between Huntly and Kennethmont on 7 September 1982.
Nikon F 85 mm Nikkor
Kodachrome 25 1/250, f3.5

Right. The whisky distillery at Dalwhinnie sets the Highland scene for class 47/4 No 47481 heading north with a Motorail train for Inverness on 8 September 1982. Just 6 miles to the south is Drumochter summit which at 1484 ft is the highest on the BR network.
Pentax 6 × 7 150 mm Takumar
Agfa R100S 1/250, f4.5

Apart from the 03 and 08 shunters, the English Electric class 20s are probably the least widely travelled diesel locomotives. Except for occasional summer duties on passenger trains to the Lincolnshire resort of Skegness, they are usually confined to trip and short distance freight workings in Central Scotland, Lincolnshire, South Yorkshire and the East Midlands. The comparatively new station of Alfreton and Mansfield Parkway, situated about one mile to the south of the site of Westhouses station, provides the setting for this study of Nos 20004 and 20044 heading south with a coal train on 25 August 1978.
Nikon F   85 mm Nikkor
Kodachrome 25   1/250, f3.5

Beyond Glenfinnan the West Highland extension from Fort William to Mallaig is one of the most scenic BR branch lines. Superb seascapes and loch scenery are set against majestic mountains as the line twists and turns through numerous tunnels and viaducts on gradients as steep as 1 in 40. In 1983 a daily service of four passenger trains each way was provided, with Eastfield class 37s the usual motive power. Freight traffic was almost non-existent, the occasional tanker of oil being attached to the rear of one of the passenger trains. On 3 June 1983, the 1630 from Fort William, pictured here in the pouring rain near Lochailort, ran as a mixed with class 20 No 20148 providing most unusual motive power.
Pentax SP   50 mm Takumar
Kodachrome 25   1/125, f2.2

In 1982 one of the few remaining regular passenger diagrams for class 25 haulage was the summer Saturday only Nottingham–Llandudno. On 27 May, the first day of the 1978 service, No 25213 leaves Derby on the last leg of the return journey to Nottingham. The train is routed through Chester and Crewe requiring reversal at Derby, a straightforward exercise now that it is, since 1983, dmu operated.
Nikon F   135 mm Nikkor
Kodachrome 25   1/250, f4

The surviving freight only branches of the North Staffordshire Railway to Caldon Low and Oakamoor in the Churnet Valley are rarely visited by enthusiasts. Class 25 diesel-electrics usually provide the motive power for the daily (weekdays only) service, operating in tandem on the stiff grades beyond Leek Brook Junction. The station at Wall Grange, closed to passengers in May 1956 and now a private residence, is passed by Nos 25160 and 25161 double-heading a heavy trainload of sand on 1 June 1979.
Leica M3   50 mm Summilux
Kodachrome 25   1/250, f3.8

Opposite. A scene once commonplace on the Midland main line, coal hauls between the coalfields of the East Midlands and South Yorkshire and the capital. Here one of the original 'Peaks', No 44005 *Cross Fell*, heads a lengthy rake of empty coal wagons along the down slow near Glendon Junction on 22 April 1975. (*Hugh Ballantyne*)
Leica M3   50 mm Summicron
Kodachrome II   1/500, f2.8

Above. In the eight years since this photograph was taken the railway scene at Kentish Town has changed beyond recognition. Indeed only the Victorian hotel on the skyline remains unaltered. A completely modernised station, 25 kV emus and HSTs present the modern British Rail image. 'Peak' No 45130 heads an up express on 21 May 1975.
Leica M3   90 mm Tele Elmarit
Kodachrome 25   1/250, f3.5

Above. On 17 April 1981 'Peak' No 45056 failed totally at Smardale while working the 1150 Glasgow Central–Nottingham. The photographer took the driver by car to Kirkby Stephen signal box to summon help in the form of No 47191 from Carlisle. Some 90 minutes late the train continued its journey south and is seen here crossing the embankment at Waitby.

Nikon F   85 mm Nikkor
Kodachrome 25   1/250, f4

Opposite. On two weekends in June 1983, due to engineering work at Winsford WCML Anglo-Scottish expresses were diverted through Stockport, Manchester (Oxford Road) and Eccles, rejoining the main line at Lowton Junction, Newton le Willows. In glorious summer weather No 47568 takes No 86239 *L S Lowry* and the 0945 Euston–Glasgow Central through Ordsall Lane, Salford on 19 June. (*David Nixon*)
Pentax 6 × 7   200 mm Takumar
Ektachrome 200   1/500, f5.6

GRANADA TV

40 192
40 073

Opposite. A varied selection of motive power including 45029, 40073, 40192 and 20046 take a well earned rest at Tinsley TMD on 27 January, one of the numerous days of inactivity in 1982 resulting from the industrial action of ASLEF members.
Nikon F   85 mm Nikkor   Kodachrome 25 1/125, f5.6

Right. Seven almost brand new class 24s, Nos D5000/2/3/5/6/10/13 and an 08 shunter are strange bedfellows for a motley selection of Southern Region steam locomotives at Hither Green shed on 2 May 1959. (*R C Riley*)
Agfa Silette   50 mm Solagon   Kodachrome I 1/125, f5.6

Below. A rose among thorns? Class 40 No D218 (40018) *Carmania*, complete with nameplate and newly acquired full yellow nose panels, takes it easy at the north end of Carnforth shed between two class 5 steam locomotives in May 1968. The buildings still stand today as part of the privately owned 'Steam-town' complex, but unfortunately are rarely host to 'Whistlers'.
Exakta Varex IIa   50 mm Pancolar Kodachrome II   1/125, f3.5

This particularly interesting photograph, taken at Stratford on 7 April 1963, features eight of the ten class 23 1100 hp 'Baby Deltics', Nos D5900/2/3/4/6/7/8/9. At this time they had been temporarily taken out of service after only three years of work on secondary duties out of Kings Cross. After modification they were reinstated in 1965 and finally withdrawn in 1968.

(Trevor Owen)
Leica M2   50 mm Summicron
Kodachrome II   1/125, f4.8

Clayton Type I Nos D8532 and D8534 double-head a heavy oil train between Carnforth and Silverdale on the morning of 26 July 1968. The photographer well recalls his disappointment that the train was not steam hauled – time has since tempered his judgement!

Exakta Varex IIa   50 mm Pancolar
Kodachrome II   1/250, f4

Opposite. There is little doubt that at the time of writing the ever popular English Electric class 40s are the focus of attention of modern traction enthusiasts. Few are diagrammed for express passenger work but during 1982 they made occasional appearances at Liverpool Lime Street, usually deputising for class 47s. On 11 September No 40013 was in charge of the four coach 1115 Barrow in Furness–Liverpool seen here negotiating Olive Mount cutting near Edge Hill.
Pentax 6 × 7
150 mm Takumar
Ektachrome 200
1/250, f6.3

Right. For many years the holiday trains from Glasgow to Scarborough have been a focus of interest for North East enthusiasts. Class 40s were regular performers, typified by this picture of No 40059 heading south from King Edward Bridge West Junction, Gateshead, on 16 July 1977.
Nikon F
85 mm Nikkor
Kodachrome 25
1/250, f4

Opposite. Among the latest in the long line of diesel multiple units is the class 140, a four-wheel lightweight vehicle based on the Leyland National bus body and powered by a Leyland 205 hp power unit. The prototype cars Nos 55500/1 have seen experimental service on a number of rural branches and cross-country lines and in 1982 they enjoyed an extensive period of work on the Central Wales line.

Here the pair are seen forming the 1500 Swansea–Shrewsbury–Crewe on 20 August 1982 as they near the summit of the climb from Landore to Cockett tunnel.
Pentax 6 × 7   105 mm Takumar
Ektachrome 200   1/500, f5.6

Above. Pre-grouping Great Northern somersault semaphore signals are now almost extinct, although in 1983 a few remained in service on the Boston to Skegness line and in sidings at both Sleaford and Lincoln. This splendid example at Roxton sidings was photographed on 13 September 1979 but just two months later it was replaced by a standard upper quadrant. The train, a Derby lightweight class 108 two car dmu in the rather attractive refurbished livery, is the 1511 New Holland Pier–Cleethorpes.
Leica M3   90 mm Tele Elmarit
Kodachrome 25   1/250, f4

Although the class 87 5000 hp 25 kV electric locomotives are to date the ultimate development of their genre, their duties on the WCML are not confined to high speed express passenger work. On 1 September 1982 No 87033 *Thane of Fife* was caught by the camera making a rather uncharacteristic cautious descent of Shap with an empty cement train.
Nikon F   85 mm Nikkor
Kodachrome 25   1/250, f3.5

Today's motive power and yesterday's rolling stock. Despite the comparative longevity of this 1964-built locomotive, 25 kV ac electric traction holds out the best long term hope for the survival of busy main line railways. However, there is no longer a place for the short wheelbase vacuum-braked mineral wagons seen here on 25 April 1982 behind No 85039 at Winwick Junction, running from Crewe Basford Hall to BSC Ravenscraig with coal from Holditch Colliery.

(Robert Osborne)
Canon AE/1   Canon 70–150 mm zoom
Kodachrome 64   1/250, f5.6

Opposite. Class 37 Nos. 37281 and 37186 leave a trail of dust over the Wiltshire countryside as they roll along at 45 mph on the descent from Hanging Langford towards Wilton Junction, Salisbury on 14 April 1983. Note that the leading wagon is sheeted over, no doubt to reduce the ingress of particles into the locomotives.
Nikon F   85 mm Nikkor
Kodachrome 25   1/250, f3

Above. The English Electric Type 3 class 37 diesel-electric locomotives were certainly one of the more successful designs introduced as part of the 1960s traction modernisation programme. Some 23 years after the building of the first example, all but one are still in service on duties ranging from passenger work on the West Highland to mundane coal hauls in the Welsh Valleys. In this scene Nos 37168 and 37211 doublehead an iron ore train westbound from Immingham Docks past the factory and quarry of Singleton Birch & Co at Melton Ross, Humberside on 2 February 1983.
Pentax 6 × 7   150 mm Takumar
Ektachrome 200   1/500, f5.6

Right. A train which used to be keenly watched by enthusiasts in Scotland was the 1038 Glasgow Queen St–Perth and the 1228 return working. Although only a 4- or 5-coach consist, the train was usually doubleheaded by a newly repaired locomotive from St Rollox Works with a standby coupled inside. In this scene an immaculate class 27 No 27063 leading No 47163 were captured on film as they approached Gleneagles on the outward journey on 3 September 1982. (*David Nixon*)
Pentax 6 × 7
200 mm Takumar
Ektachrome 200
1/500, f5.6

Opposite. On trial from Derby Works Peak No D58 (45043), resplendent in its then newly acquired blue livery, heads past Buxworth signal box up the bank towards Chinley in October 1966. The signal box has since been demolished and the tracks furthest from the camera, the up and down slow lines, lifted.
Exakta Varex IIa
80 mm Biometer
Kodachrome II

1T35

The humble 08 shunters are undoubtedly the Achilles heel of present day locospotters. They may be found anywhere over virtually the whole BR network and often they contrive to hide away in almost disused sidings in inaccessible locations. Equally they are a challenge to the photographer; really first class pictures of 'Gronks' at work are few and far between. In this photograph No 08183 lives up to the reputation as it keeps well out of the public eye during shunting movements at Masborough South on 26 August 1977.
Leica M3
90 mm Tele Elmarit
Kodachrome 25
1/125, f5.6

The railway scene at Ipswich has changed little in recent years but major developments are imminent. The days of the visually attractive but archaic semaphore signals are numbered, whereas plans to electrify the main line through to Norwich are well advanced. Here class 47/4 No 47566 approaches East Suffolk Junction with the 1430 Liverpool Street–Norwich on 3 August 1982. In the yard 08 No 08661 toys with a string of Freightliner wagons while Stratford based No 47117 awaits its next call to duty.
Nikon F   85 mm Nikkor
Kodachrome 25   1/250, f3.5

Above. Class 56 No 56010 passes Harbury Blue Circle Cement Works at Greaves Sidings north of Fenny Compton with a northbound empty Didcot–Staveley mgr on 9 April 1983.
Pentax 6 × 7   150 mm Takumar
Ektachrome 200   1/500, f4.5

Opposite. Framed by the branches of a dead tree at Elmton and Cresswell class 56 No 56085 wheels a string of merry-go-round hoppers round the curves towards Worksop on 26 March 1982. Somewhat surprisingly few of the many surviving railways in the East Midlands now carry passenger traffic. This former Midland line links major centres of population at Worksop, Mansfield and Nottingham but passenger trains were withdrawn in 1964.
Nikon F   85 mm Nikkor
Kodachrome 25   1/250, f4

No 3205, a 4-CAP emu formed in 1982 by the combination of a pair of 2-HAP units, leaves a rather deserted Eastbourne as the 1203 to Brighton on 28 March 1983. The generous platform accommodation provides a reminder of more prosperous times at this south coast terminus.

Pentax 6 × 7   *150 mm Takumar*
Ektachrome 200   *1/500, f5.6*

Vauxhall, just 1¼ miles from Waterloo station, is at the heart of the London commuter country south of the capital, where the ubiquitous Southern Region third rail emu reigns supreme. In this scene two generations of stock are illustrated; class 421 4-CIG No 7340, forming a down express for Portsmouth, overtakes a class 508 unit bound for Effingham Junction on 16 April 1983. (*John S Whiteley*)
Olympus OM1   85 mm Zuiko
Kodachrome 64   1/250, f5.6

Opposite. Freight trains don't come any shorter than this! Class 40 No 40185 toys with one four-wheeled van as it emerges from Standedge tunnel into a Yorkshire winter wonderland at Marsden on 16 December 1981.
Nikon F   85 mm Nikkor
Kodachrome 25   1/250, f4.5

Above. Sub-zero temperatures appear not to daunt the antics of enthusiasts aboard the F & W 'Napier North Eastern' railtour on 10 December 1981. 'Hoover' No 50010 *Monarch* was photographed passing Burton Salmon, near Pontefract, on the last lap of the run to York, where now preserved 'Deltic' No 55002 took the train on to Scarborough.
Nikon F   85 mm Nikkor
Kodachrome 25   1/250, f4

Opposite. Cogload Junction, east of Taunton, is one of the more interesting locations on the Western Region. Here the main lines from Bristol and Westbury converge, and as can be seen from this photograph the superbly engineered layout permits relatively high speed movements in all directions. Here class 47/0 No 47089 *Amazon* takes the Bristol line with a northbound freight on 6 August 1980. Note in the train consist the nuclear flask containing radioactive waste from the power station at Hinkley Point.
Nikon F   85 mm Nikkor
Kodachrome 25   1/250, f4

Above. The autumn tints of the moors overshadowing the Lune Gorge near Tebay complements the two-tone green livery of class 47 No D1524 heading south over Dillicar troughs with a steel tube train in November 1967. (*Derek Huntriss*)
Pentax Spotmatic   50 mm Takumar
Kodachrome II

'Western' diesel-hydraulic No. 1012 *Western Firebrand* passes Hungerford with a Merehead–Ardingly stone train on 11 June 1975. Note the rake of empties, headed by an unidentified class 47, standing in the now lifted down loop. (*John Vaughan*)
Nikkomat FTN   50 mm Nikkor
Agfa CT18   1/500, f4.5

Except when undergoing trial runs between Manchester and Derby the Beyer Peacock-built Type 3 class 35 diesel-hydraulics never wandered far from the Western Region. Unique in many respects the locomotives gained the nickname 'Hymek', an abbreviation of their hydraulic-mekydro transmission system. In this scene No D7044 takes the Westbury line at Fairwood Junction with a freight on 12 July 1963. (*Hugh Ballantyne*)
Voigtlander CLR   50 mm Skopar
Agfa CT18   1/500, f4.5

Opposite. The former Lancashire and Yorkshire line over Copy Pit, linking the Lancashire towns of Burnley, Blackburn and Preston with West Yorkshire industrial centres along the Calder Valley, was once a major rail artery. Indeed in steam days banking engines were always on hand at Todmorden to assist trains up the hill through Portsmouth to the summit. Today the occasional freight train, excursion and summer Saturday traffic to and from Blackpool are the only reasons for the line's continued existence. Here rail enthusiast passengers on the 1353 (SO) Blackpool–Sheffield are treated to the dual delights of relatively rare haulage and route mileage as class 37 No 37228 approaches the summit on 24 July 1982.
Pentax 6 × 7   200 mm Takumar
Ektachrome 200   1/500, f6.3

Below. The railway along the coast of North Wales is intensively used on summer Saturdays by holiday trains serving the resorts of Rhyl, Prestatyn, Colwyn Bay and Llandudno. The hillside above Penmaenrhos tunnel is a particularly attractive location for railway photography with panoramic views of the line set against a backdrop of Colwyn Bay and the Great Orme. On a rather misty 15 August 1981 class 47/4 No 47539 climbs away from Colwyn Bay at the head of the 1022 Holyhead–Euston.

Present day visitors to this spot may be disappointed to find that the railway has been realigned; the spacious foreground is occupied by civil engineering contractors who are busy constructing a new coastal road by-pass.
Nikon F   85 mm Nikkor
Kodachrome 25   1/250, f3.5

Present day travellers on the WCML north of the Border to Glasgow may well be unaware of the fierce grades of Beattock; electric-hauled expresses travel uphill almost as fast as down. Judging by the exhaust of the steam banker, the 1 in 74 bank was evidently a tough proposition for English Electric class 40 No D294 (40094) at the head of a down oil train on 31 May 1966. The photographer is to be congratulated on the neat tree felling operation in the foreground! (*Hugh Ballantyne*)

Voigtlander CLR   50 mm Skopar
Agfa CT18   1/500, f4

At the time of writing, traffic over the full length of the Settle and Carlisle line has been reduced to four daily passenger trains and future prospects seem particularly bleak. Saturday 2 April 1983, however, was a day of intense activity since the line carried all WCML traffic re-routed because of a bridge replacement at Tebay. Hundreds of spectators and photographers lined the route in weather which ranged from warm spring sunshine to raging blizzard. In this scene 40074 is reduced to 20 mph on the last pitch of the climb to Ais Gill with the 17-vehicle empty Perth–Red Bank vans.
Nikon F   85 mm Nikkor
Kodachrome 25   1/250, f3.8

The third rail Bury–Manchester Victoria emus operating at 1200 Volts dc were pioneered by the Lancashire and Yorkshire Railway and continue to be unique in the BR network. The most obvious distinction from their Southern Region cousins is the sideways contact of the current pick-up shoes with the live rail. The safety of this system, particularly for permanent way staff, is obvious and one wonders why it was not adopted elsewhere. Class 504 emu No M77175 passes Queens Road, Cheetham with a service bound for Manchester on 25 September 1982.
Pentax 6 × 7
105 mm Takumar
Agfa CT18
1/250, f4.5

This delightful period study of 4-SUB electric multiple unit No 4508 photographed in Clapham cutting on 24 May 1958 recalls the early days of Southern Railway electrification. This particular unit was constructed from ex-SECR steam stock as a 3-SUB set when built in 1928. Many sets were augmented to four-car formations in the immediate post-war years by the addition of an all steel construction trailer. Note the lion-on-wheel emblems. (*R C Riley*)

Agfa Silette   50 mm Solagon   Kodachrome I   1/250, f2.8

In complete contrast, a modern class 303 25 kV suburban emu set forming a Wemyss Bay–Glasgow Central service, hugs the banks of the Clyde near Langbank on 15 April 1982.

Nikon F   85 mm Nikkor
Kodachrome 25   1/250, f4

The twelve class 47/7 diesel-electrics are modified examples of the standard Brush design for push-pull operations north of the Border, principally on the Edinburgh–Glasgow Inter-City services. Here No 47705 *Lothian* finds itself in unusual surroundings as it propels a rake of five Mk III coaches and DBSO, forming the 1330 Glasgow Central–Edinburgh, through Shotts on the former Caledonian Glasgow–Edinburgh line on 11 April 1982. On that weekend the usual North British link was closed because of a bridge replacement at Linlithgow.
Nikon F   85 mm Nikkor
Kodachrome 25   1/250, f4

Above. A delightfully vintage railway scene at Masborough South Sidings near Rotherham on 25 August 1977. In an almost model like setting class 46 No 46020 ambles past the Midland Railway signal box with a southbound freight train of ageing four-wheeled unfitted wagons – a sight soon destined to disappear from the mod- ern BR scene.
Leica M3   90 mm Tele Elmarit
Kodachrome 25   1/250, f4

Opposite. Judging by the exhaust, class 25 No 25078 found it hard work to keep its lengthy mixed freight train on the move as it climbed the 1 in 130 through Wormit on the south bank of the River Tay on 5 September 1980. Scotland TMDs have now totally lost their allocations of class 25s, while their numbers south of the bor- der are rapidly dwindling. (*Mrs D A Robinson*)
Pentax 6 × 7   105 mm Takumar
Ektachrome 200   1/500, f5.6

The mercury in the thermometer dips almost out of sight as the sun sets on a very cold 12 December 1981. The simultaneous appearance of three locomotive-hauled trains at Skipton these days is rather unusual. On this occasion the passenger trains were stabled ecs waiting to return to Keighley to pick up visitors to the KWVR while the 'Peak' had arrived earlier in the day with the daily Heysham Moss–Haverton Hill ammonia tanks. (*Robin Lush*)
Nikon F3   85 mm Nikkor
Kodachrome 25   1/4, f4.5

The steam heating equipment of No 31184 seems to be working efficiently as it prepares to depart from Sheffield with the 2332 to Manchester on 2 May 1983. The corresponding train on the following day, hauled by 31214, met with a serious accident in the Hope Valley when it struck a derailed cement tanker at about 60 mph.

Nikon F   85 mm Nikkor
Kodachrome 25   1½ minutes, f4, tripod

Apart from a brief period of service on GE and GN lines in the Home Counties in the late 1950s the North British class 21 diesel-electrics, and their class 29 re-engined derivatives, were exclusively associated with secondary duties in Scotland.

In this scene No D6123 heads past Hilton Junction signal box on the last stage of the run into Perth with an express from Glasgow Buchanan St on 10 August 1965. The class became extinct in 1971. *(Gavin Morrison) Zeiss ContaFlex 50 mm Agfa CT18*